SHE

BOOKS BY ROBERT A. JOHNSON

He: Understanding Masculine Psychology, Revised Edition

She: Understanding Feminine Psychology, Revised Edition

We: Understanding the Psychology of Romantic Love

Inner Work: Using Dreams & Active Imagination for Personal Growth

Ecstasy: Understanding the Psychology of Joy

SHE

Understanding Feminine Psychology

Revised Edition

ROBERT A. JOHNSON

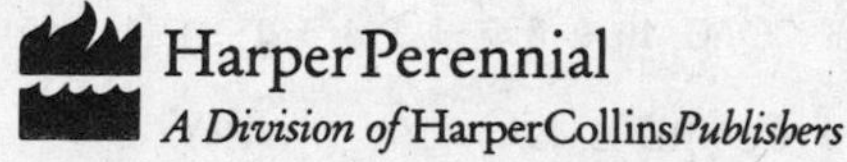

HarperPerennial
A Division of HarperCollins*Publishers*

To John A. Sanford
certainly the godfather
of this work

This revised edition is published by arrangement with Mills House, P.O. Box 8147, Berkeley, California, 94707.

REVISED EDITION

LIBRARY OF CONGRESS CATALOG CARD NUMBER 89-45098

ISBN 0-06-055179-8

ISBN 0-06-096397-2 (pbk.)

89 90 91 92 93 CC/FG 10 9 8 7 6 5 4 3 2 1

07 08 09 10 CC/RRD-H 40 (pbk.)

Acknowledgments

My great appreciation to Glenda Taylor and Helen Macey for the heroic tasks of transcriptions, additions, editing, and typing the lecture tapes into readable form for the original edition of this book. My gratitude to the many people of the parish of St. Paul in San Diego for their contributions to the evolution of this book and to the many readers and friends who encouraged my thinking and made possible this revised edition.

Contents

Introduction

The Greek myth of Eros and Psyche is one of the most instructive stories there is on the feminine personality. It is an ancient, pre-Christian myth, first recorded in classical Greek times, having had a long oral tradition before that; yet it is relevant for us today.

This is not as strange as it might seem. Since human biology appears to be the same today as it was in Greek times, so also the unconscious psychological dynamic of the human personality is similar. Basic human needs, both physiological and psychological, have remained stable although the form in which those needs are satisfied may vary from time to time.

This is why it is instructive to go to the earliest sources to study the basic patterns of human behavior and personality. Their portrayal is apt to be so direct and simple we cannot fail to learn from them.

Also we can begin to see the changes and variations peculiar to our own time.

THE ROLE OF THE MYTH

Myths are rich sources of psychological insight. Great literature, like all great art, records and portrays the human condition with indelible accuracy. Myths are a special kind of literature not written or created by a single individual, but produced by the imagination and experience of an entire age and culture and can be seen as the distillation of the dreams and experiences of a whole culture. They seem to develop gradually as certain motifs emerge, are elaborated, and finally are rounded out as people tell and retell stories that catch and hold their interest. Thus themes that are accurate and universal are kept alive, while those elements peculiar to single individuals or a particular era drop away. Myths, therefore, portray a collective image; they tell us about things that are true for all people.

This belies our current rationalistic definition of myth as something untrue or imaginary. "Why, that is only a myth; its not true at all," we hear. The details of the story may be unverifiable or even fantastic, but actually a myth is profoundly and universally true.

A myth may be a fantasy or a product of the imagination, but it is nonetheless true and real. It depicts levels of reality that include the outer rational world as well as the less understood inner world.

This confusion concerning the narrow definition of reality may be illustrated by the thinking of a small child after a nightmare. A parent may say, to be comforting, "It was only a dream; the monster was not real." But the child is unconvinced, and rightly so. To him it was real, as alive and real as any outer experience. The monster he dreamed about was in his head and not in his bedroom, but it had, nonetheless, an awesome reality, with power over the child's emotional and physical reactions. It had an inner reality for him that cannot and should not be denied.

Myths have been carefully studied by many psychologists. C. G. Jung, for example, in his studies of the underlying structure of the human personality, paid particular attention to myths. He found in them an expression of basic psychological patterns. We hope to do the same with our study of Eros and Psyche.

First we must learn to think mythologically. Powerful things happen when we touch the thinking which myths, fairy tales, and our own dreams bring to us. The terms and settings of the old myths are strange; they seem archaic and distant to us, but if we listen to them carefully and take them seriously, we begin to hear and to understand. Sometimes it is necessary to translate a symbolic meaning, but this is not difficult once we see how it can be done.

Many psychologists have interpreted the Eros and Psyche myth as a statement of the feminine personality. Perhaps it would be wise at the very beginning of this study to say that we are speaking of femininity wherever it is found, in men as well as in women. To confine this story to women's personalities alone would be to limit it severely.

Dr. Jung, in one of his most profound insights, showed that, just as genetically every man has recessive female chromosomes and hormones, so, too, every woman has a group of masculine psychological characteristics that make up a minority element in her. The man's feminine side Dr. Jung called the *anima;* the woman's masculine side he called the *animus.*

Much has been written about the anima and animus and we will have more to say about both of them later. At this point, whenever we speak of the feminine aspects of the Eros and Psyche myth, we are speaking not only about women, but also about the man's anima, his feminine side. The connection may be more obvious to a woman, since femininity is her major psychological quality, yet there will also be something of a parallel to the interior feminine aspect of a man's psychology.

The Birth of Psyche

Our tale begins with the line—Once there was a Kingdom. From this we know that we will be given vision and insight into that kingdom, which is our own inner world. If you listen to the old language of the tale you will see into that inner realm, seldom explored by the modern rational mind. A gold mine of information and insight is promised by a few words—Once there was a Kingdom.

THE STORY BEGINS

There is a king, a queen, and their three daughters. The two eldest are ordinary princesses, not very remarkable.

The third daughter is the very embodiment of the inner world and even bears the name Psyche, which means *soul.* She will take us on a journey to the inner world. She is as much of the mythic kingdom as she is of the earthly kingdom.

Do you know these three in yourself? Who can be unaware of the ordinary part of one's self and that special unearthly inner self who does so badly in the ordinariness of everyday life?

So great was the power of this extraordinary princess that people began saying, "Here is the new Aphrodite, here is the new goddess who will take the place of the old one, drive her from her temple, and entirely supercede her." Aphrodite had to bear the insult of seeing the ashes of the sacramental fires in her temples grow cold and the cult of this new slip of a girl take her place.

Now, Aphrodite was the goddess of femininity who had reigned since the beginning—no one knew how long. For her to see the rise of a new goddess of femininity was more than she could bear! Her rage and jealousy were apocalyptic and the whole course of our story is determined at this moment. To stir the rage or demand change of a god or goddess is to shake the very foundations of one's inner world!

THE MYTHIC ELEMENTS

The origins of the two goddesses, Aphrodite and Psyche, are interesting. Wielding a sickle, Cronus, the youngest and craftiest son of Uranus, the god of the sky, severed his father's genitals, and flung them into the sea thus fertilizing the water and Aphrodite was born. Aphrodite's birth was immortalized by Botticelli in his magnificent painting, the *Birth of Venus:*[1] she, in all her feminine majesty, is being born upon a wave, standing on a shell. This is the divine origin of the feminine principle in its archetypal form, which may be vividly contrasted with the human birth of Psyche who was said to have been conceived by dewdrops that fell from the sky. What curious language! But this language is rich in psychological insight if you can hear its archaic, timeless message.

The difference between these two births, if properly understood, reveals the different natures of the two feminine principles. Aphrodite is a goddess born of the sea: she is primeval, oceanic in her feminine power. She is from the beginning of time and holds court at the bottom of the sea. In psychological terms, she reigns in the unconscious, symbolized by the waters of the sea. She is scarcely approachable on ordinary conscious terms; one might as well confront a tidal wave. One can admire, worship, or be crushed by such archetypal femininity but it is extremely difficult to relate to it. It is Psyche's task, from her human vantage point, to do just that—to relate and soften the great oceanic, archetypal feminine. This is our myth.

[1]Venus is the Roman name for Aphrodite.

Every woman has an Aphrodite in her. She is recognized by her overwhelming femininity and vast, impersonal, unrelatable majesty.

There are marvelous stories about Aphrodite and her court. She has a servant who carries a mirror before her so that she may constantly see herself. Someone continually makes perfume for her. She is jealous and will stand no competition whatsoever. She is constantly arranging marriages and is never satisfied until everyone is busily serving her fertility.

Aphrodite is the principle of mirroring every experience back into our own consciousness. As man is occupied with expansion and exploration and finding that which is new, Aphrodite is reflecting and mirroring and assimilating. Aphrodite's mirror is symbolic of a most profound quality of the goddess of love. She frequently offers one a mirror by which one can see one's self, a self hopelessly stuck in projection without the help of the mirror. Asking what is being mirrored back can begin the process of understanding, which may prevent getting stuck in an insoluble emotional tangle. This is not to say there are not outer events. But it is important to realize and understand that many things of our own interior nature masquerade as outer events when they should be mirrored back into our subjective world from which they sprang. Aphrodite provides this mirror more often than we would like to admit. Whenever one falls in love, sees the god or goddess-like qualities in another, it is Aphrodite mirroring our immortality and divine-like qualities. We are as reluctant to see our virtues as our faults and a long period of suffering generally lies between the mirroring and the accomplishment. Psyche takes just such a long journey between her falling in love with Eros and the discovery of her own immortality.[2]

This Aphrodite is the great mother goddess as seen through the eyes of her future daughter-in-law. When a woman mediates beauty and grace to the world, often it is the Aphrodite or Venus energy at work. But when Aphrodite is confronting her daughter-in-law she is jealous, competitive and determined to set out hurdles for Psyche at every turn. This drama of mother-in-law and daughter-in-law is acted out in every culture and is one of the psychic irritants which can contribute so much to a young woman's growth. For a young woman to cope with her mother-in-law's power system is to attain feminine maturity. She is no longer that dewdrop which came so naively into the world and into her marriage.

It is embarrassing for a modern, reasonably intelligent woman to discover her Aphrodite nature and the primitive, instinctive tricks it can play. Aphrodite

[2]I am indebted to Betty Smith for this insight.

often shows her tyrannical side and thinks her word is law.

Naturally, when a new kind of femininity appears on the stage of evolution, the old goddess will be irate. She will use any means at her disposal to down an opponent. Every woman knows this through her own sudden regressions to her Aphrodite nature; a woman is a terrifying figure when she falls prey to it. It is a rare and intelligent household where, in her sudden eruptions, Aphrodite can be called by her true name and that sublime energy put to its real use.

Aphrodite energy is a valuable quality. She is in the service of personal development and wields her terrible power to make those around her grow. When it is time for growth, the old ways and the old habits must welcome the new. The old way seems to hinder the new growth at every point, but if you persevere, this way will bring a new consciousness to birth.

There is a story about the first elephant born in captivity. At first its keeper was delighted, but then he was horrified when the other elephants in the compound gathered in a circle and tossed the new baby to each other around the circle. The keeper thought they were killing it, but they were only making it breathe.

Often, when new growth occurs, the most dreadful things seem to happen, but then we see that they were exactly what was required. Aphrodite, who is criticized at every turn, does what is necessary to make Psyche's evolution possible. It is easy to be optimistic after the fact, but it is devilishly painful while it is happening. There is a sort of inner chaotic evolutionary warfare happening during this time. The old way, the Aphrodite nature, is regressive. It pulls a woman back into unconsciousness, while at the same time it forces her forward into new life—sometimes at great risk. It may be that evolution could be accomplished in another way; or it may be that at times Aphrodite is the only element that can bring about growth. There are women, for example, who might not grow unless they have a tyrant of a mother-in-law or stepmother.

THE COLLISION

Much of the turmoil for a modern woman is the collision between her Aphrodite nature and her Psyche nature. It helps to have a framework for understanding the process; if she can see what is happening, she is well on her way to a new consciousness.

The Youth of Psyche

Having seen something of the nature of Aphrodite, the older, more primitive level of femininity, let us look at the new expression of the feminine. Unlike Aphrodite, who was born from the sea, Psyche was born when a dewdrop fell on the land. This change from the ocean of Aphrodite to the land of Psyche is a progression from the early oceanic feminine quality to a new form which is more human-like. From oceanic proportions we move to a smaller more comprehensible scale.

Psyche's nature is so magnificent, so innocent, so unworldly, so virginal that she is worshipped; but she is not courted. This is an utterly lonely experience and poor Psyche can find no husband.

In this sense, there is a Psyche in every woman, and it is an intensely lonely experience for her. Every woman is, in part, a king's daughter, too lovely, too perfect, too deep for the ordinary world. When a woman finds herself lonely and not understood, when she finds that people are good to her but stay just a little distance away, she has found the Psyche nature in her own person. This is a painful experience and women are often aware of it without knowing its origin. To be caught in this aspect of the feminine character is to remain untouched and unrelated.

All manner of nonsense goes on when a woman tries to bring her Psyche nature into the everyday give-and-take of relationship. If the Psyche nature is a large part of a woman, she has a painful task on her hands. She bursts into tears and says, "But nobody understands me." And it is true! Every woman has this quality within her; it makes no difference what her station in life may be. If you see this quality and can touch it in a woman, the great beauty and divinity of a Psyche can be made conscious in her and a noble evolution begins.

If a woman is very beautiful, the problem is compounded. Marilyn Monroe is a touching example; she was worshipped far and wide and yet had great difficulty relating closely to any one person. Finally she found life intolerable. Such a woman is the carrier of a goddess-like quality, an almost unapproachable perfection that finds no place in the ordinary human realm of relationship. You can set in motion the evolution required of Psyche if you understand this dynamic.

I once saw a film in which two horribly disfigured people in an institution fell in love with each other. Through the magic of fantasy each became infinitely beautiful to the other and a love affair went on between these two handsome, beautiful people. At the end of the movie, the camera blurred back to show the two originally disfigured faces; but the audience knew where they had been; they had seen the god and goddess within, which were stronger than the outer reality of disfigurement. This shows the breach between the interior goddess and the exterior everydayness that is the heart of our story.

THE MARRIAGE

Psyche is the despair of her parents because, while her two older sisters have happily married neighboring kings, no one asks for Psyche's hand. Men only worship her. The king goes to an oracle, who happens to be dominated by Aphrodite, and she, irate and jealous of Psyche, has the oracle give a terrible prophesy! Psyche is to be married to Death, the ugliest, the most horrible, the most awful creature possible. Psyche is to be taken to the top of a mountain, chained to a rock, and left to be ravished by this dreadful creature, Death.

Oracles were unquestioned in Greek society; they were taken as absolute truth. Psyche's parents, believing, made a wedding procession, which was a funeral cortege, took Psyche as instructed, and chained her to the rock at the top of the mountain. Mixed together were floods of tears, wedding finery, and funeral darkness. Then the parents extinguished the torches and left Psyche alone in the dark.

What can we make of this? Psyche is to be married—but to Death! In truth the maiden does die on her wedding day; an era of her life is over and she dies to many of the feminine elements she has lived thus far in her life. Her wedding is her funeral in this sense. Many of our wedding customs are actually funeral ceremonies carried over from primitive times. The groom comes with his best man and friends to abduct the bride; the bridesmaids are the protectors of the virginity of the bride. A battle, in ritual form, is carried out and the bride cries as is befitting the death of a section of her life. A new life opens for her and the festivities are to celebrate the new power as bride and matriarch.

We are not sufficiently aware of the dual aspect of marriage and try to see it only as white and joyous; the dying to an old part of life should be honored or the emotions will surface later in a less appropriate form. For example, some women may experience a fierce resentment toward marriage months or even years later.

I have seen pictures of a Turkish wedding party in which boys of eight or nine each had one foot bound to their thigh and were hopping on one leg. This was to remind everyone that pain was present at the wedding as well as joy.

In African weddings, unless the bride arrives with scars and wounds, it is not a valid wedding. Unless she has been abducted there is no true wedding. If the sacrificial element of a wedding is given its due, the joy of the marriage is possible. Aphrodite does not like maidens to die at the hands of men. It is not her nature to be carried off by a man. So the Aphrodite in a woman weeps at the ending of her maidenhood. Aphrodite plays her paradoxical role of demanding the wedding but resenting the loss of the maiden. These echoes from long ago still lie deep in us and are best honored by conscious ceremony.

Here again we observe the paradox of evolution. It is Aphrodite who condemns Psyche to death but who is also the matchmaker who brings about the very wedding she is opposing. The forward evolution toward marriage is accompanied by a regressive tug of longing for the autonomy and the freedom of things as they were before.

I once saw an insightful cartoon that summed up the archetypal power of a wedding. It showed the thoughts of each of the parents during the wedding. The father of the bride is angry at that fellow who is audacious enough to snatch his darling away from him; the father of the groom is triumphant at the supremacy of the males of the community; the mother of the bride is horrified at the beast who is carrying away her child; the mother of the groom is angry at the vixen who has seduced her son away from her. Many of the ancient archetypes, those embedded patterns of thought and behavior laid down in the unconscious of the human psyche through countless years of evolution, were depicted in the cartoon. If we do not observe them at appropriate times they will intrude later and cause much trouble.

Eros

In order to destroy Psyche, as she wished to do, Aphrodite engages the assistance of her son, Eros, the god of love. Eros, Amor, and Cupid are various names that have been given to the god of love. Since Cupid has been degraded to the level of valentine cards, and Amor has been shorn of his dignity, let us use the name Eros for this noble god.

Eros carries his quiver of arrows and is the bane of everyone on Olympus; not even the gods escape his power. Yet Eros is under the thumb of his mother who instructs him to enflame Psyche with love for the loathsome beast who will come to claim her, thus ending Psyche's challenge to Aphrodite. One of Aphrodite's characteristics is that she is constantly regressive. She wants things to go back where they were; she wants evolution to go backward. She is the voice of tradition, and ironically, it is this very tendency that carries our story forward in its evolution.

There are many levels from which to view Eros. He may be seen as the outer man, the husband, or the male in every relationship; or he may be seen as the principle of union and the harmony that is the culmination of our story. Eros is not only sexuality: remember that he aims his arrows at the heart, not at the genitals. We will speak of these aspects of Eros as our myth continues.

THE WEDDING OF DEATH

Eros goes to do his mother's bidding, but just as he glimpses Psyche, he accidentally pricks his finger on one of his own arrows and falls in love with her. He decides instantly to take Psyche as his own bride and asks his friend, the West Wind, to lift her very gently down from the top of the mountain into the Valley of Paradise. The West Wind does this, and Psyche, who was expecting Death, finds herself in a heaven-on-earth instead. She does not ask Eros any questions but luxuriates in her unexpected good fortune. Eros comes to Psyche, and even beautiful as he is, he is death to her. All husbands are death to their wives in that they destroy them as maidens and force them into an evolution toward mature womanhood. It is paradoxical, but you can feel both gratitude and resentment toward the person who forces you to begin down your own path of growth. The oracle was right; a man is death to a woman in an archetypal sense. When a man sees an anguished look on his partner's face, this is a time to be gentle and cautious; it may be that she is just waking up to the fact that she is dying a little as maiden. He can make it easier for her at this moment if he will be gentle and understanding.

A man rarely understands that marriage is death and resurrection both for a woman, since he has no exact parallel in his own life. Marriage is not a sacrificial matter to a man, but there is much of that element in a woman's experience. She may look at her husband in horror one day because she realizes she is bound in her marriage as he is not. She is even more profoundly bound if there are children. She may resent this, but not to be caught in this way by life is an even worse death.

There are women of fifty who have never been to the Death mountain, though they may be grandmothers. The dewy quality is not off the world for them even in middle age. There are also young girls of sixteen who know that experience, have been through it and survived it and have a terrifying wisdom in their eyes.

These things do not happen automatically at any particular age. I knew a girl of sixteen who had a baby. She went off to have it privately and quietly and gave the baby away in adoption so that she never saw it. She came back and nothing had happened to her; she had not learned anything of the Death mountain. Several years later she married, and if anybody could be called virginal, she had that quality. Psychologically she had not been touched, even though she had been through the experience of childbirth.

The Eros in each woman terminates her naivety and childlike innocence at vastly different times in life; it is not just when she marries. Many girls are through it very early in life, which is a cruel experience; others never experience it at all.

Marriage is a very different experience for a man than for a woman. The man is adding to his stature; his world is getting stronger, and he has risen in stature and position. He generally does not understand that he is killing the Psyche in his new wife, and that he must do this. If she behaves strangely, or if something goes dreadfully wrong, or there are many tears, he usually doesn't understand that marriage is a totally different experience for her than for him. A woman takes on a new stature in her marriage but not until she has been through the Death mountain experience.

THE GARDEN OF PARADISE

Psyche finds herself in a magnificent paradise. She has everything one could wish. Her god-husband, Eros, is with her every night and puts only one restriction on her; he extracts from her the promise that she will not look at him and will not inquire into any of his ways. She may have anything she wishes, she may live in her paradise, but she must not ask to know or see him. Psyche agrees to this.

Nearly every man wants this of his wife. If she will not ask for consciousness and do things his way there is perfect peace in the house. He wants the old patriarchal marriage where the man decides all the important issues, the woman agrees, and there is peace. Most men harbor the hope that things will go in this manner and for a little while there is the possibility that marriage will be like this.

This is likely an echo of some primitive patriarchal structure in which the woman is subject to the man. There are still remnants of this patriarchal world in our modern customs, for example, when a woman bears the man's name. Eros insists that she not ask any questions, never see him; these are the conditions of the patriarchal marriage.

Every immature Eros is a paradise-maker. It is adolescent to carry a girl off and promise her that she will live happily ever after. That is Eros in a secretive stage; he wants his paradise, but no responsibility, no conscious relationship. There is a bit of this in every man. The feminine demand for evolution and growth—and most growth comes from the feminine element in the myths—is a terrifying experience to a man. He wants just to remain in paradise.

Listen to lovers build a paradise! The talk and vocabulary is of another world, the paradise world. It is a brief preview of a true paradise that will be attained much later by very hard work. One can not criticize such a preview, but an onlooker knows the first glimpse of paradise will not be stable or long-lasting.

There is something in the unconscious of a man that wishes to make an agreement with his wife that she shall ask no questions of him. Often his attitude toward marriage is that it should be there for him at home but it should not be an encumbrance. He wants to be free to forget about it when he wants to focus elsewhere. This is a great shock to a woman when she discovers this attitude in her man. Marriage is a total commitment for a woman; it is not so all encompassing for a man. I remember a woman who told me she cried for days when she discovered that their marriage was only one aspect of her husband's life though it was the primary fact of hers. She had discovered her husband in his Eros, paradise-making nature.

PARADISE LOST

All paradises fail. Each one has a serpent in it that demands the opposite of the peace and tranquility of the Garden of Eden.

The serpent quickly appears for Psyche's paradise in the form of her two sisters, who have been mourning her loss—though not with deep sincerity. They hear that Psyche is living in a garden paradise and that she has a god as a husband. Their jealousy knows no bounds! They come to the crag where Psyche had been chained and call down to her in the garden, send their best wishes, and inquire about her health.

Psyche naively reports all this to Eros. He warns her over and over that she is in great danger. He tells her that if she pays attention to her inquiring sisters, there will be a disaster. And if Psyche continues unquestioning, her child will be a god and immortal; but if she breaks her vow of not questioning, the child will be born a girl and a mortal. Worse than this, Eros will leave her if she ever begins questioning him.

Psyche listens and again agrees to ask no questions. The sisters call again and finally Psyche extracts permission from Eros to let them come for a visit. Soon after, the sisters are wafted down from the high crag by the West Wind, and are deposited safely in the lovely garden. They admire everything and are entertained lavishly. Of course they are consumed with envy and jealousy at what has happened to their young sister. They ask many questions and Psyche, in her naivete, describes her husband through her own fantasy though she has never seen him. She heaps extravagant presents upon her sisters and sends them home.

Eros warns again and again, but the sisters come back. This time Psyche, forgetting what she had told them before, tells a different fantasy about her husband. When the sisters return home they discuss this and brew up a venomous plan. On a third visit they will tell her that her husband is actually a serpent, a loathsome creature, and that when her baby is born, he plans to devour both mother and child!

The sisters also have a plan to save Psyche from this horrible end. They advise Psyche to get a lamp, put it in a covered vessel, and have it ready in the bedchamber. She is to take the sharpest knife available and have it beside her on the couch. In the middle of the night, when her husband is fast asleep, she must expose the lamp, see her loathsome husband for the first time, and sever his head with her knife. Psyche quickly falls under the spell of this advice and prepares herself to unmask her terrible husband.

Eros comes to the couch after dark and falls asleep beside Psyche. In the night she takes the cover off the lamp, grasps the knife, stands over her husband, and looks at him for the first time. To her utter amazement and bewilderment, and now overwhelmed with guilt, she sees that he is a god, the god of love, the most beautiful creature in all of Olympus! She is so shaken and terrified by this that she thinks of killing herself at her terrible mistake. She fumbles with the knife and drops it. She then accidentally pricks herself on one of Eros' arrows and falls in love with the husband she has seen for the first time.

She jostles the lamp and a drop of oil from it falls on Eros' right shoulder. He wakes in pain from the hot oil, sees what has happened and, being a winged creature, takes flight. Poor Psyche clings to him and is carried a little way just far enough to be taken from the paradise garden. She soon falls to the earth exhausted and desolate. Eros lights nearby and says that she has disobeyed, broken her covenant, and destroyed the paradise garden. He tells her, as he had warned, her child will be born a mortal and a girl. He will go away, punishing her by his absence. Then he flies away to his mother, Aphrodite.

THE MODERN DRAMA

This is a drama replayed countless times in many marriages. What does this archaic, poetic, mythic language tell us about woman and her relationship to man—both inner and outer?

The sisters are those nagging voices within, and often without, who do the double task of destroying the old and bringing consciousness of the new. Mid-morning coffee-klatches are often the scene of the two sisters brewing up destructive plots. The two sisters are often at work doing their double duty of challenging the old patriarchal world and urging each other on to a consciousness that will cost more than they realize. We are likely to pay a Promethean cost for the consciousness we so bravely demand.

The questioning sisters are a frightening spectacle, for, though they are the harbingers of consciousness, there is the danger that you can be caught in their stage of development and remain destructive for the rest of your life. Just as you can stay on the mountain of Death and see men as purveyors of disaster, so you can also be caught in the stage of the two sisters and destroy anything that a man tries to create.

A woman is likely to go through a bewildering series of relationships with her partner. He is the god of love, and he is death on the top of the mountain; he is the unknown one in paradise, and he is the censoring one when she demands consciousness. And finally he is the god of love at the summit of Olympus when she comes to her own goddesshood. All this is bewildering to a man. Small wonder that he peers around the door a little gingerly when he comes home each day to see which role is waiting for him. Add to this his own anima involvements and it makes a complex story—but a beautiful one.

The sisters are the demand for evolution from an unexpected source. They may be Psyche's shadow. Dr. Jung described the shadow elements in a personality as those repressed or unlived sides of a person's total potential. Through lack of attention and development, these unlived and repressed qualities remain archaic or turn dark and threatening. These potentialities for good and evil, though repressed, remain in the unconscious, where they gather energy until finally they begin to erupt arbitrarily into our conscious lives, just as the sisters came into Psyche's life at a critical moment.

If we see ourselves consciously as pure loveliness and gentleness only, as Psyche did, we are overlooking this dark side and it may emerge to push us out of our self-satisfied, naive paradise into new discoveries about our true nature.

Dr. Jung said that the demand for growth in consciousness often comes from the shadow. So the sisters, those less than lovely and imperfect parts of Psyche, serve her well.[3]

[3]C. S. Lewis treats this aspect of the myth with genius—Psyche's naive identification with her own loveliness and the less lovely sisters reaction to it—in his book, *Till We Have Faces.*

The Confrontation

Eros has worked as hard as he can to keep Psyche unconscious. He promised her paradise if she would not look at him or question him. In this way he sought to dominate her.

A woman often lives some part of her life under the domination of a man in outer life, and if she is alert enough to avoid this she may then fall under the domination of her inner man, her animus. The chronicle of a woman's life can be described in her struggle and evolution in relation to the masculine principle of life—whether she finds it outwardly in a human male or within herself as animus. There is an exact parallel in the life of a man as he struggles to gain some intelligent relationship with the feminine principle of life—whether he finds it through a woman or in the heroic struggle around his inner woman, his anima. Outer or inner, this is much of the drama of life.

Though there are endless variations that make up the individuality of life, the coming-to-terms with the masculine element takes a predictable course. A young woman is likely to touch masculinity first as father, then as the devourer in her marriage to death, then as Eros who promises paradise if she will not ask questions. Later she will find him as the god of love that he truly is. Within or without this drama takes so much of our conscious energy!

A woman's autobiography is likely to contain vivid chapters on her falling in love, the discovery and loss of the paradise garden, and, God willing, the rediscovery—as wonderful as it's first promise—of the garden in maturity.

The honeymoon of courtship, which is the paradise garden, claims us first. There Psyche finds herself in the most lovely of tranquil gardens where her every wish is accomplished. This is the paradise-garden, the Garden of Eden, the place of perfection. We wish this might last forever, but every garden has a serpent or shadow figure who brings the tranquility to an abrupt halt.

THE TOOLS

The shadow urges a woman to question the paradise garden and gives her some wonderful and terrible tools for her purpose. There is a lamp, hidden at first, which is her ability to see what *is.* This is her capacity for consciousness. Light is always the symbol of consciousness, whether it be in the hands of man or a woman. A woman's natural consciousness is of a unique and beautiful kind, a lamp. It burns the oil of the earth or of the fruit and gives a particularly warm, gentle, soft light. There is not the hard intensity of sunlight in it but the gentle feminine warmth of nature's light. Luminea Natura is one of its names.

The other tool is a knife, very sharp. Of these tools Psyche uses only one. She never uses the other, and I think there is sage advice in the myth in this respect. A woman gently shedding light on a situation produces miracles; a woman with a knife in her hands would kill. Transform or kill? This is a critical choice, especially for a modern woman. If the knife comes first there will probably be much damage. If the lamp comes first there is a chance of intelligence and growth. If she wields her tools carefully she can bring about a miracle of transformation—nothing less than the showing forth of the god, Eros in his true light. She can be justly pleased that her light produced the miracle. Much of a man's mute yearning for a woman is his need for her light to show him—as well as her—his true nature and godhood. Every woman holds this terrible-wonderful power in her hands.

What is the lamp, and what does it show? At his

best, a man knows who he is, and he knows he has a god, a magnificent being, somewhere within him. But when a woman lights the lamp and sees the god in him, he feels called upon to live up to that, to be strong in his masculine consciousness. Naturally he trembles! Yet he requires this feminine acknowledgment of his worth. Terrible things happen to men who are deprived of the presence of women—inner or outer—for usually it is the presence of woman that reminds each man of the best that is in him.

During World War II, there were isolated groups of men stationed in the Aleutian islands. They were deprived of "R and R," rest and relaxation, because of transportation problems due to their isolation. None of the entertainment groups went near them. More than half of these men suffered nervous breakdowns. They would not shave, cut their hair or do the things necessary to keep up their morale. It was because there was no woman, no Psyche looking upon Eros, to remind them of their worth.

If a man is discouraged, a woman can give him a glance or a talisman and restore him to his sense of value. There seems to be a peculiar vacant spot in a man's psychology here. Most men get their deepest conviction of self-worth from a woman, wife, mother, or if they are highly conscious, from their own anima. The woman sees and shows the man his value by lighting the lamp.

I was sitting in on a family quarrel once when a woman was wielding her knife vigorously. Far down on the list of her husband's transgressions was the accusation that he often got home from the office late. He said, "Don't you understand that I stay at that stupid office for you, to earn and care for the family?" The woman collapsed. She had heard something. The lamp had replaced the knife. He said, "I wouldn't go to the office except for you. I hate the office. I only go there to work for you and the children." There was a suddenly a new dimension in that marriage. The woman brought forth her lamp and looked at what was. And she liked what she saw.

A man depends largely on woman for the light in the family as he is not well equipped at finding meaning for himself. Life is often dry and barren for him unless someone bestows meaning on life for him. With a few words, a woman can give meaning to a whole day's struggle and a man will be so grateful. A man knows and wants this; he will edge up to it, initiate little occasions so that a woman can shed some light for him. When he comes home and recounts the events of the day, he is asking her to bestow meaning on them. This is the light-bearing quality of a woman.

The touch of light or consciousness is a fiery experience and often stings a man into awareness; this is partly why he fears the feminine so much. A huge proportion of man's bantam rooster behavior is a futile effort to hide his fear of the feminine. It is mostly the woman's task to lead a man to new consciousness in relationship. It is almost always the woman who says, "Let's sit down and talk about where we are." The woman is the carrier of growth in most relationships. A man fears this but he fears, even more, the loss of it.

We can understand the function or meaning of the oil from Psyche's lamp in two ways. We can speak of oil on troubled waters and also of being boiled in oil. In a man's hazy appreciation of the feminine the two are not always easily separated.

A blustery old Jewish patriarch once consulted me concerning the lack of life in his household. The children were gone, he was retired, and gloom had settled over the enervated household. I sensed what had gone wrong and asked about the ceremonies of the household. "Oh, we gave those up eons ago; they have no meaning." I instructed the man to ask his wife to light the Sabbath candles the next Friday evening.[4] "Rubbish!" he cried. But I insisted and wondered what he would recount the next week when I saw him again. "I don't know what happened but when I asked my wife to light the Sabbath can-

[4]In an orthodox Jewish household the Sabbath begins at sundown on Friday evening. It is custom for the woman to light the Sabbath candles at the beginning of the Sabbath.

dles she burst into tears and did as I asked. The household has been a different place ever since!" Two things had happened: ceremony had been restored to that household, and the woman had been given her ancient right to bear the lamp of soft light which warms, animates, and brings meaning.

Few women understand how great is the hunger in a man to be near femininity. This should not be a burden for a woman and she will not have to bear this in such a solitary manner all of her life. As a man discovers his own inner femininity, he will not rely so heavily on the outer woman to live this out for him. But if a woman wishes to give a most precious gift to a man, if she would truly feed his greatest masculine hunger (a hunger which he will seldom show but which is often there), she will be very feminine when her man is mutely asking for that precious quality. It is especially true that when a man is in a mood he needs true femininity from his woman so that he may get his bearings and be a man again.

Love or In Love

Aphrodite has accomplished her task of evolution of consciousness in the most extraordinary way! By what seems a series of blunders and mistakes a wonderful story of development has taken place! Aphrodite, bless her devious soul, in jealousy, sent Psyche to her Death wedding to a hideous monster on the mountain top. She sent her son, the god of love, to arrange the marriage; but Eros pricked his finger on his own arrow of love and fell in love with Psyche himself. Then in a terrible moment of revelation Psyche also pricked her finger on one of his arrows of love and fell in love with the god of love!

What is this quality of "In Love" which seems to have the power to set aside the dictates of fate and produce such miracles? It is necessary to differentiate two terms, *love* and *in love,* before we can begin to unravel this mystery.

To *love* someone is a human experience bonding

one in a human way to another being. It is seeing that person truly, and appreciating him or her for the ordinariness, failures, and magnificence of human personality. If we can ever cut through the fog of projections in which we live so much of our life, and look truly at another person, we can perceive an ordinary creature as magnificent. The trouble is that we are blinded by our own projections; we rarely see another clearly in all of his or her depth and nobility. Such love is durable and bears up under the ordinariness (a word which derives from *orderedness*) of everyday experience. A friend lovingly describes it as "stir the oatmeal love." It finds its fulfillment in everyday events and does not need superpersonal dimensions.[5] One serves, relates, blunders, safeguards, and lives in the every-day-ness of the stream of human life.

When one falls *in love* he has touched a superhuman level of experience and is instantly wafted away into a god-like realm where human values are superseded. It is as if we were caught in a whirlwind from heaven and tumbled into a realm in which ordinary human values are obliterated. If *love* is 110 volt usable house current, *in love* is 100,000 volts of superhuman energy that can not be contained in any ordinary household environment. *In love* is of the gods and

[5]See Robert A. Johnson, *We: Understanding the Psychology of Romantic Love.* (San Francisco: Harper & Row Publishers, Inc., 1983), for further discussion of this subject.

goddesses and is beyond time and space.

It has been said that Psyche is the first mortal who ever looked at a god in his true splendor and lived to tell the tale. This is the heart of our story; a mortal fell in love with a god and stayed true to her humanity and faithful to her love. The sublime ending of the story is a direct result of Psyche being true to herself and to her love.[6]

Let us try an experiment; imagine that all of the people on earth are gone except one other person and yourself. Search out that person in the course of the day and see how valuable they now seem to you. For a little time that person is a true miracle incarnate. It is this heaven-concentrated-into-a-single-point which is the experience of falling in love. This miracle is true of any human, but we see it only occasionally and for a brief time in someone. This is a far different order from the "stir the oatmeal" love which is durable and keeps a stable household. (If someone had told me twenty years ago I would be equating love and durability I would have been shocked and angry. But middle age brings small bits of wisdom.)

Both Eros and Psyche prick their finger on the magic arrow and are transported to the *in love* realm.

[6]See Robert A. Johnson, *Ecstasy* (San Francisco: Harper & Row Publishers, Inc., 1987), in which Semele, a mortal woman, fell in love with Zeus and was incinerated for her mistake.

Miracles follow—and inevitably, much suffering. Psyche is rescued from her Death marriage; Eros is unmasked as the god which he is; Psyche is banned from her paradise; and Eros is sent flying away to his mother in pain. The *in love* experience shatters human tranquility but sets about a great evolutionary energy.

In earlier times the experience of being touched by the gods took place in a religious context; we have moved away from such settings for our profound experiences. Almost the only place where ordinary people are touched by the gods in our time is in romance. Falling in love is the experience of looking through that person and seeing the god or goddess who stands behind. No wonder we promptly become blind when we fall in love. We walk right by the real person and focus on something greater than any ordinary human being. Psychologically speaking, this is saying that prior to the time of our myth, if you touched an archetype, you were simply obliterated. The myth tells us that henceforth, and under certain circumstances, when mere mortals undergo an archetypal experience, they may survive it, but will be radically changed by it. I think this is the touchstone of our story. A mortal touches something of supermortal dimensions—and lives to tell the tale. Within this context, one can see what it means to be touched by the arrows of the god of being-in-love. One can see the profound experience that it is, the transposition of levels involved. This is the incredible, explosive experience of falling in love.

Asian people do not have a tradition of falling *in love.* They go to their relationships quietly, undramatically, untouched by the arrows of Eros. Marriages are arranged. Traditionally the man does not see his bride until the ceremony is over and the garlands of flowers are lifted. Then he takes her home and follows a carefully prescribed pattern for newly married couples. He keeps the energy we experience as *in love* for the temple where the gods and goddesses bear this great power for him.

Our story is about a woman who was touched by something far greater than ordinary human experience. The rest of the myth tells us how she survived this divine touch.

The Dismissal of Eros

When Eros was unmasked as a god, the revelation caused him to suffer extreme pain. The paradise was over, for he was shown to be what he truly is—not the god of the death-marriage or the maker of paradise—but the very embodiment of love itself. This is even more difficult and painful than to find out that he was an imposter or less than he had promised. How strange that the best of all possibilities is so painful! Though it is totally unexpected, this proves to be true in many life situations. A teacher of mine told me a story to illustrate this: a very excitable young man came for his tutorial after about six months of analysis. "Toni, it is too terrible!" "What, is there bad news?" replied Toni, equally excitable. "Toni, just leave me alone; it is too awful." "What, tell me, tell me!" "Toni, my neurosis is gone and how am I going to live?" The moral of the story is clear. To lose one's old way of adaptation is very bad news even if it is replaced by something far better. Both Eros and Psyche are profoundly wounded when the next stage of their evolution appears—even though it is a vast improvement for both.

It is ironic that the moment you fall in love with someone, you must acknowledge that person's utter uniqueness and thus their separateness. Then we become immediately aware of the distance, the separation, and the difficulty of relationship. There is generally a terrible feeling of inferiority in both men and women when they find that their companion is a god or goddess. Loneliness and isolation follow quickly.

Eros makes good his threat; Psyche will have a baby girl instead of a boy and it will be a mortal rather than a god. And Eros will leave Psyche. This is to say that humanness and ordinariness will supercede the paradise garden.

When this is enacted in the external world it too often becomes a sad drama early in marriage. When she discovers that he is not the paradise-maker she had expected and uncovers his ruse of invisibility, both suffer a severe shock. This is the potential for a dramatic rise in consciousness but it registers as extreme pain. Both are expelled from the paradise garden and set firmly into human proportions. This can be a fine moment because people make much better humans than they do gods or goddesses. But it does cause emotional suffering.

Eros flies away to his mother, Aphrodite, and figures very little in the rest of the story. Poor Psyche is left to journey all on her own, though she has more helpers than she realizes. Even Aphrodite, that mother-in-law ogre, is caring for her in an astringent way. During this experience the man may leave his marriage and go home to his parent's house. Or if he does not leave physically, he may have unaccountable bouts of silence, be perfunctory and unavailable emotionally. He has gone home to mother—at least to his interior mother complex if not his actual mother. Then Aphrodite reigns supreme in the woman's consciousness.

If we view Eros as the woman's animus, her interior masculine side, we may say that Eros held Psyche in a state of unconscious animus possession in paradise until she lit the lamp of consciousness. Then, when his true identity is discovered, he flew back into the inner world where he belongs.

THE ANIMUS

Dr. Jung has said that the anima and animus function most effectively for us as mediators between the conscious and unconscious parts of the personality. When Eros returns to the inner world of Aphrodite, he is able to mediate for Psyche with Aphrodite,

Zeus, and the other gods and goddesses of the inner, archetypal world. As we shall see, he is able to send help to Psyche at critical times in her development by using natural, earthy elements such as the ants, the eagle, and the reeds.

If a woman is to evolve past feminine adolescence she must break the unconscious domination of her subordinate, largely unconscious, masculine component which often dictates her relationship to the outer world. For her to evolve, the animus, consciously recognized as such, must take up a position between the conscious ego and the unconscious inner world where he can act as mediator, an essential help to her. He then can open up a true spiritual life for her. A woman in a state of animus possession, that is with her animus mediating between her and the outer world, is not consciously aware of her animus at all. She believes her behavior is arising from her animus and is her own ego-determined choice. In fact, her ego is taken over in these instances by the animus. When a woman lights the lamp of consciousness, she sees the animus, quite correctly, as separate from her ego. Like Psyche, she is usually overwhelmed. The animus seems so potent and godlike, and her conscious self so worthless and helpless by comparison. This is a desperate and dangerous moment for her. After she goes through the awesome shock of first recognizing her animus and being overwhelmed with her own inadequacy, she is then equally in danger of being overwhelmed by his grandeur. If she sees that she has a godlike element within the result is exhilarating, much like a peak experience. She is now in great danger of "falling in love with love himself."

If you can negotiate this development and keep afloat between the extremes of man-as-death and man-as-god, paradise and banishment, exhilaration and despair—you can begin the truly human task of developing consciousness. The promise rings true and faithful: if you can bear to see your man for what he truly is then light the lamp which only you can provide. You will find your man to be a god—probably not in the paradise sense which you hoped for, but in the Olympian sense, which is much greater. I know no greater promise in life.

This event in Psyche's life is something like Parsifal's first sight of the grail castle.[7] Parsifal sees a magnificent world beyond belief, but he is not to remain there. Likewise, Psyche loses Eros almost immediately upon discovering his true, magnificent nature.

[7]See Robert A. Johnson, *He: Understanding Masculine Psychology, Revised Edition,* (New York: Harper & Row Publishers, Inc., 1989), for masculine parallels to this experience.

The Suffering of Psyche

Psyche immediately wants to drown herself in a river. As she faces each of a series of difficult tasks, Psyche wants to kill herself. Does this not point toward a kind of self-sacrifice, the relinquishing of one level of consciousness for another? Almost always in human experience the urge toward suicide signals an edge of a new level of consciousness. If you can kill the right thing—the old way of adaptation—and not injure yourself, a new energy-filled era will begin. When a woman is touched by an archetypal experience, she often collapses before it. It is in this collapse that she quickly recovers her archetypal connection and restores her inner being. This constellates the helpful elements in her deeper self. A woman does this in a different way from a man. While he probably has to go out seeking a heroic task and kill many dragons and rescue fair maidens, she generally has to withdraw to a very quiet place and remain still. Paradox heaped upon paradox, she may find that she did embrace death in her marriage; yes, death to an old way of living.

It is bewildering to a man to discover the degree to which a woman has control over her feelings and inner world, a capacity unknown to most men. She can enter at will a deep place within herself where healing and balance are restored. Most men have no such control over their feelings or inner life. Many women presume this same differentiation in their men and are hurt that they are not capable of the same degree of sensitivity.

Being in love is likely to tear you into bits; but this has its creative possibilities also. If you maintain the strength and courage, out of this dismemberment may come a new consciousness of uniqueness and worth. That is a very difficult way to go, but perhaps there is no other way for some temperaments. It seems to be our chief western way of reconnecting with the archetypal energies that we call gods or goddesses.

The best way to solve this dilemma is to stand absolutely still, and that is what Psyche finally does. Once she gets past her suicidal feelings, she sits very quietly. If you have been dazzled out of your wits, if you have been knocked totally out of orbit, it is best to keep very still. This is the moment in the Christian liturgy of the Eucharist when, "Here we offer and present unto Thee ourselves . . . a living sacrifice."

A woman has a profound capacity to be still, perhaps the most powerful act any human being can make. She is required to go back to a very still inner center every time something profound happens to her. This is a highly creative act but must be done correctly. She is to be receptive, not passive.

It is possible to translate being *in love* into loving. This is the history of a successful marriage. Our western marriages begin *in love* and, hopefully, make the transition into loving. That is the basic theme of our story; it begins as a collision between a mortal and a goddess, between two levels of being, between humanness and a superhuman quality. Both have to learn, generally painfully, that the superhuman quality can not be lived out on a human level.

I remember a James Thurber cartoon in which a middle-aged couple is quarreling and the husband hurls at the wife, "Well, who took the magic out of our marriage?"

When touched by a god or goddess, what are we to do? That question is largely unanswered in our culture. Most people suffer and endure the fading of the godlike vision of the beloved, settle down into a humdrum middle age, and think that their vision of a divine quality was all a bit foolish anyway. The feminine alternative to this self-defeating and depressing end to being *in love* occupies the rest of our story.

PSYCHE ALONE

To be touched by a godlike experience is to become open to learning a godlike consciousness, godlike in a Greek, Olympian sense. Once you have been touched in this way you can never return to simple, carefree, unconscious ways. When a westerner is touched by being *in love,* now one of the only ways we are visited by the gods anymore, a road of evolution can be traveled that has consciousness as its goal.

The task for a woman is to translate the pain and suffering of a tragic love affair into the mundane steps of personal development.

Psyche goes to the river to give herself up, perhaps with the wrong superficial motives but with the right instincts.

Pan, the cloven-footed god, is sitting by the river with Echo in his lap. He sees that Psyche is about to drown herself and dissuades her.

But why Pan? He is the god of being beside one's self, wild, out of control, near-madness, which the ancients thought so highly of and we regret so bitterly when it seizes us. We derive our word *panic* from his name. It is this very quality that saves Psyche. If we can find the god Pan in the right way, that is if we can be driven out of ourselves into something higher, that energy can be used for our benefit. To be driven into something lower, such as suicide, would be the wrong way.

A fit of weeping is a Pan experience. Although it is humiliating (and that word means to be near the humus or earth), dissolving into tears can take you quickly to something greater than yourself. It is Aphrodite's power of evolution that brings you to this point and she will take you the next step of the way without fail.

Pan tells Psyche that she must pray to the god of love, the god who understands when someone is inflamed by his arrows. It is a nice irony that you must go to the very god who has wounded you to ask for relief.

Being the god of love, Eros is the god of relationship. It is the essence of the feminine principle—whether in a man or woman—to be loyal to Eros, to relationship. Always follow the path that will keep relationship with the anima or animus, for it is with this you have to live most intimately.

In order to find Eros, however, Psyche must confront Aphrodite, for he is in her power now. Psyche rebels at this and goes to the altars of many goddesses instead of to Aphrodite. She is rejected time after time since none of the gods or goddesses will risk offending Aphrodite. Her wrath would be too much to risk!

There is an instructive parallel here between Psyche and Parsifal. Psyche goes from altar to altar, and finally to Aphrodite's, the correct one; Parsifal is red-knighting, fighting heroic battles, conquering dragons. Whether you are a man or a woman, these dynamics of the masculine and feminine principles are important to remember. Men and women both have feminine/masculine characteristics and must choose the right tool for the specific task they confront.

Psyche finally goes to Aphrodite's altar, for it is almost always the case that whatever has wounded you will also be instrumental in your healing.

Aphrodite can not resist giving a tyrannical speech which reduces Psyche to the status of a scullery maid, a low place indeed. Women almost always have to endure a period of Aphrodite-domination, a time when they feel lower than the lowest. Aphrodite then delivers four tasks to Psyche; these are to be her redemption.

The Tasks

The tasks Aphrodite lays out for poor Psyche constitute one of the most profound psychological statements in literature. The modern mind cries out, "Yes, thank you for all the theory, but what do *I do*". This part of our myth lays out a more coherent pattern of development for the feminine principle than anything else available. The fact that the story is drawn from an era long ago in our psychic history does not make it less applicable, but rather honors its universality and timelessness. Countless prescriptions exist for the masculine way; but our story is one of the few feminine ways in our heritage.

After Psyche has survived Aphrodite's vitriolic tirade she receives instructions so specific as to thrill one. But why should we have to go to Aphrodite for this? Nowhere else! Psychological events come in a package; naivete, problem, waiting, and solution are neatly done up in one coherent structure.

THE FIRST TASK

Aphrodite shows Psyche a huge pile of seeds of many different kinds mixed together and tells her she must sort these seeds before nightfall or the penalty will be death. Then Aphrodite sweeps off grandly to a wedding festival. Psyche is left with this impossible task. She weeps and decides on suicide again.

An army of ants comes to her rescue. They sort the seeds with great industry and accomplish the task by nightfall. Aphrodite returns and begrudgingly concedes that for a good-for-nothing Psyche has done tolerably well.

What a beautiful bit of symbolism; a pile of seeds to sort! In so many of the practical matters of life, in the running of a household, for example, or its parallel in a professional life, the challenge is to make form and order prevail. Whether it is the cry from down the hall, "Mom, where is my other sock?" or the shopping list, or a new outline for that manuscript—all this is sorting, order and form. Without that essential task of establishing form there would be chaos.

When a man makes love to a woman, he gives her seeds in vast number. She has to choose one and begin the miracle of birth. Nature in her Aphrodite character produces so much! Woman in her sorting capacity must choose one seed and bring it to fruition.

Most cultures try to eliminate this sorting and ordering through custom and law. They stipulate what a woman shall do and this saves her from having to sort. Monday is for washing, Tuesday is for ironing, etc. We are free people and have no such safeguards. A woman must know how to differentiate, how to sort creatively. To do this she needs to find her ant-nature, that primitive, chthonic, earthy quality which will help her. The ant-nature is not of the intellect; it does not give us rules to follow; it is a primitive, instinctive, and quiet quality, legitimately available to women.

Each woman has her own proficiency in this sorting attribute. Tasks can be done in a kind of geometric way, the nearest one first, or the one closest to a feeling value first. In this simple, earthy way you can break the impasse of too-muchness.

It is easy to overlook another dimension of the sorting process—the inner one. Just as much material comes from the unconscious demanding to be sorted as comes from our modern too-much-with-us outer world. It is the special provence of a woman to sort in this inner dimension and protect herself and her family from the inner floods which are at least as damaging as the too-muchness of our outer world. Feelings, values, timing, boundaries—these are wonderful sorting grounds which produce such high values. And they are special to woman and femininity.

One may view a marriage as two people standing back to back, each protecting the other in a particular way. It is the feminine task to protect not only herself but her man and her family from the dangers of the inner world; moods, inflations, excesses, vulnerabilities, and what used to be called possessions. These are things a woman's genius can manage much better than a man's. Usually he has his own task in facing the outer world and keeping his family safe. There is a particular danger in the modern attitude in which both people face the outer world, both spend their time in outer things. This leaves the inner world unprotected and many dangers creep into the household through this unprotected quarter. Children are particularly vulnerable to this unprotectedness.

When a marriage begins the partners are like two discrete circles overlapping a little. The division between the two is great and each has specific tasks. As the marriage partners grow older, each learns a bit of the other's genius, and finally the two circles overlap more and more.

Dr. Jung tells the story of a man who came for treatment of an ailment. When asked to share his dreams he replied that he never dreamed but that his six-year-old son dreamed most vividly. Dr. Jung asked him to record his son's dreams. The man brought his son's dreams for several weeks and then suddenly began dreaming himself. The son's overblown dreams stopped immediately! Dr. Jung explained that the man, unwittingly—for he had fallen into the usual modern collective attitude towards such things—had failed to take care of an important dimension of his own life and the son had been obliged to bear that burden for him. If you wish to give your children the best possible heritage, give them a clean unconscious, not your own unlived life, which is hidden in your unconscious until you are ready to face it directly.

Generally it is the woman who tends these inner fires, but in this example it was the father's task that had fallen onto the child. When we speak of masculine and feminine it must remain clear that we are not talking exclusively about male and female. A man's feminine side may take on the task we usually think of as belonging to a woman and vice versa.

THE SECOND TASK

The second of Psyche's tasks, arrogantly and insultingly set out by Aphrodite, is to go to a certain field across a river and gather some of the golden fleece of the rams pastured there. She is to be back by nightfall, on pain of death.

Psyche must be very brave, perhaps foolhardy, if

she is to accomplish this dangerous task, for the rams are very fierce. Once more she collapses and thinks of suicide. She goes toward the river which separates her from the field of the sun-rams, intending to throw herself in. But just at the critical moment the reeds on the river's edge speak to her and give her advice.

The reeds, humble products of the place where water meets land, tell Psyche not to go near the rams during the daylight hours to gather wool. If she did she would immediately be battered to death. Instead, she should go at dusk and take some of the wool that has been brushed off by the brambles and low hanging boughs of a grove of trees. There she will get enough of the golden fleece to satisfy Aphrodite without attracting the attention of the rams. Psyche is told not to go directly to the rams or try to take the golden fleece by force; the rams would be very dangerous if approached in this way. She is to approach these dangerous bull-headed, aggressive beasts only indirectly.

Masculinity often looks ram-like to a woman when it comes time for her to assimilate a little of that quality into her interior life. Imagine a very feminine woman at the beginning of her life looking at the modern world and knowing that she must make her way through it. She fears that she will be killed, bludgeoned to death, or depersonalized by the ram nature of the patriarchal, competitive, impersonal society in which we live.

The ram represents a great, instinctive, masculine, elemental quality that can erupt unexpectedly as an invading complex within a personality. This power is awesome and numinous like the experience of the burning bush. Forces and powers in the depths of the unconscious that can overwhelm the conscious ego if they are not handled correctly.

Our myth gives explicit instruction on how Psyche may wisely approach the ram power. She is not to go to it in the heat of the day but at dusk; and she is to take fleece that has gathered on the twigs and branches, not directly from the rams. Too many modern people think that power is to be had only by wrenching out a handful of fleece from the back of a ram and going off in triumph in the noonday sun. Since power is such a double-edged sword, it is a good rule to take only as much as one needs—and that as quietly as possible. To underdo power is to remain dominated by interior parental voices. Overdoing power can quickly become abusive and rampage about leaving behind wreckage and destruction.

John Sanford, author and therapist, observes that if a young person takes drugs his ego may not be strong enough to withstand the massive interior experience he encounters; he may be obliterated. This would be taking on the ram-power directly or in too great of a quantity. We moderns, men and women, are grasping a ram of massive proportions that may turn on us and destroy us. Our myth cautions us to take the power we need, sacrifice what is not required, and keep power and relatedness in proportion.

The idea of having to take the remnants, just the scrapings of logos, the masculine rational scientific energy, off the boughs, may sound intolerable to a modern woman. Why should a woman have to take just a little of this quality? Why can't she simply pin down the ram, take his fleece, and leave triumphantly like a man?

Delilah did just this and made a great power play of it. She left much destruction in her wake. The Psyche myth tells us that a woman can obtain the necessary masculine energy for her purposes without a power play. Psyche's way is much gentler. She does not have to turn into a Delilah and kill a Sampson in order to obtain power.

This bit of mythology raises a very large question for modern people: how much masculine energy is enough? I think there are no limits so long as a woman remains centered in her feminine identity and only uses her masculine energy in a subsidiary way and as a conscious tool. So also with a man: he may use as much feminine energy as he can so long as he remains a man using his feminine side in a conscious way. Too much of either can cause a great deal of trouble.

THE THIRD TASK

Aphrodite discovers that, incredibly, Psyche has gathered enough of the golden fleece. In her anger she decides to cause Psyche certain defeat; she tells her that she must fill a crystal goblet with water from the Styx, a river that tumbles from a high mountain, disappears into the earth, and comes back to the high mountain again. It is a circular stream, ever returning to its source, down into the depths of hell and back up to the highest crag again. This stream is guarded by dangerous monsters, and there is no place where one can set foot near enough to the stream to get one small goblet of water from it.

True to form, Psyche collapses, but this time she is numb with defeat and cannot even cry.

Then an eagle of Zeus appears as if by magic. The eagle assisted Zeus in a certain amorous episode earlier, so the eagle and Zeus have a warm camaraderie. Zeus, now willing to protect his son Eros openly, asks the eagle to assist Psyche. The eagle flies to her in her distress and asks for the crystal goblet. Flying to the center of the stream, he lowers the goblet into the dangerous waters and fills it and brings the vessel safely back to Psyche. Her task is accomplished.

The river is the river of life and death; it flows high and low, from the high mountains down into the depths of hell. The current of the river is fast flowing and treacherous; the banks are slippery and steep. Approaching too closely, one could easily be swept off and drowned in the waters or crushed on the rocks below.

This task is telling us how the woman must relate to the vastness of life. She may take only one goblet of water. The feminine way is to do one thing and do it well and in proportion. She is not denied a second or third or tenth activity but she must take it one goblet at a time, each in good order.

The feminine aspect of the human psyche has been described as unfocused consciousness. The feminine nature is flooded with the rich vastness of possibilities in life and is drawn to all of them, usually all at once. But this is impossible; one cannot do or be so many things at once. Many of the possibilities open to us oppose each other and one must choose among them. Like the eagle, who has a panoramic vision, one must look at the vast river, focus on a single spot, and then dip out a single goblet of water.

There is a popular heresy abroad today which states that if a little is good, more is better. Following this dictum creates a life which is never fulfilling. Even while you are engaged in one rich experience, you are looking about for another. There is no contentment because future plans are always intruding on the present.

Our myth tells us that a little of a quality, experienced in high consciousness, is sufficient. As the poets tell us, we may see the world in a grain of sand. We can focus on one aspect of life, or one experience, concentrate on it, drink it in, and be satisfied. Then we can move on to whatever may follow in good order.

The crystal goblet is the container in which the water of life is held. Crystal is very fragile and very precious. The human ego may be compared to the crystal goblet; it is the container for a small portion of the vastness of the river of life. If the ego container, like the goblet, is not carefully used the beautiful but treacherous river will shatter it. Vision like an eagle to see clearly and dip into the river at the right place in the right manner is important. The ego that is attempting to raise some of the vast unconscious into human conscious life must learn to contain only one goblet of water at a time lest it be overwhelmed and the container shattered. This warns against any great plunge into the depths to bring the whole of life into focus; better one crystal goblet of water than a flood which may drown us.

The earthbound individual may look down into the crashing, swirling confusion and feel that there is no way to sort it all out. From this narrow point of view she can not see clearly enough to have a workable perspective. It is at this moment that she needs her eagle vision, which has a much broader perspective and can see the great flow of life. When the small bit of river bank looks impossible, the eagle perspective opens up the next step—probably a small step in light of normal ambition, but a necessary step for progress in personal growth.

Almost every person is overwhelmed by the too-muchness of modern life, even on a day to day basis. That is the time for the eagle view and one-goblet-at-a-time mentality.

THE FOURTH TASK

Psyche's fourth task is the most important and most difficult of all. Few women reach this stage of development and its language may seem strange and remote. If it is not your task, leave it and work at what is correct for you. For the few women who must embark on this fourth task, the information in our myth is priceless.

Aphrodite, true to form, prescribes an impossible task for a mortal. If we had to rely only on our own personal power we would never survive any of the tasks—least of all this one. But a helper appears who is the gift of the gods and makes the tasks possible.

The fourth task is Aphrodite's last test for Psyche. She is instructed to go to the underworld and ask Persephone—goddess of the underworld, the most hidden, the eternal maiden, queen of mysteries—for a cask of her beauty ointment, which Psyche is then to deliver to Aphrodite.

Psyche, seeing the impossibility of this task, goes to a high tower that she might throw herself from it and escape this terrible fate.

It is this very tower, first chosen as escape, which gives Psyche the instruction she needs; and what curious instructions they are! Psyche is instructed to go to a hidden place and there find the breathing-place of Hades opening out into a pathless way leading to the Palace of Pluto, god of the underworld. Psyche is not to go empty handed for she must earn her passage. She is to carry two pieces of barley cake in her hands, two halfpenny coins in her teeth, and sufficient fortitude to pass several difficult tests. The passage through Hades is not without its price and preparation is essential.

Psyche finds her way to the pathless path, descends to the river Styx and finds a lame man driving a lame donkey laden with sticks of wood. Some of the sticks fall to the ground and Psyche automatically, in her generosity, reaches to retrieve them for the lame man. She is forbidden to do this since it would exhaust her energies, which must be kept for the difficult task ahead. Then she comes to the ferryman, Charon, with his patched boat who requires one of the coins for passage to Hades. During the passage over the river, a drowning man begs for help from Psyche and she must refuse him. When a woman is on her way to face the goddess of the underworld she must save all her resources and not be concerned with lesser tasks.

Now in Hades, Psyche walks toward her goal and is confronted with three old women weaving the strands of fate on a loom. They ask Psyche to help but she must walk by and give them no attention. What woman can walk by the three fates and not stop to take part in the weaving of fate? But Psyche is warned that she would lose one of her barley cakes in this way and then she would have no payment for a dark passage later in the journey. Without this payment Psyche could never again return to the human world of light.

Next, Psyche confronts Cerberes, the guardian of Hades, a monstrous dog with three heads. She throws one of the barley cakes to the horrible dog and goes by while the three heads are fighting over the cake.

Finally she is in the hall of Persephone, the eternal maiden, queen of mysteries. As the tower had warned her, Psyche is to refuse the lavish hospitality Persephone offers. She accepts only the simplest food and sits upon the ground to eat it. An old law binds you to any house where you have taken hospitality and so if Psyche accepts the luxury of Persephone, she will be bound to her forever.

Psyche, in her growing wisdom and strength (for all the earlier tasks have strengthened her), passes each of these tests and asks Persephone for a cask of her beauty ointment. Persephone gives the precious cask without question, and Psyche retraces her steps. The story recounts that Persephone gives Psyche "a cask in which a mystical secret is contained." This is a clue to a perplexing question that will arise soon. She has kept the second barley cake to buy her way past the terrible dog, and she has the second coin ready for the ferryman.

The last of the instructions given by the tower proves too much for Psyche and she disobeys its wise counsel. The tower had instructed her never to open the box or to inquire into its contents. Just at the last of her journey, within sight of the light and human world, Psyche thinks within herself, "Here I have the precious beauty of Aphrodite in my hand; would I not be foolish not to look into the cask and take a tiny bit that I might adorn myself so that I would be beautiful to my beloved Eros?" This she did and found nothing in the box! The nothing issues forth as an infernal and deadly sleep. It overcomes Psyche who then lay on the path as a corpse without sense.

Eros, having recovered from his wounds, hears his beloved Psyche's distress and finds a way out of his mother's imprisonment. He flies to her, wipes the deadly sleep from her face and puts it safely back in the cask. He awakens her with the prick of one of his arrows and admonishes her for having succumbed to her curiosity, which almost killed her.

Eros instructs Psyche to proceed with her task, and she takes the mysterious cask to Aphrodite.

Eros flies straight away to Zeus and pleads his cause for Psyche. Zeus reprimands Eros for his poor behavior but finally honors him as his son and promises his help. Zeus calls all the gods together and instructs Hermes to bring Psyche to the court. Zeus announces to all the citizens of heaven that Eros' tyranny of love has gone on long enough and it is time that this young firebrand be put into the fetters of wedlock. Since Eros had chosen a bride for himself, one of most fair countenance, Zeus demands a wedding. To overcome the difficulty of uniting a god and a mortal Zeus oversees a ceremony. He gives fair Psyche a pot of immortality and instructs her to drink from it. This brings her both immortality and the promise that Eros will never depart from her again but be her everlasting husband.

There was a festival in heaven never before equalled! Zeus presided, Hermes served, Ganymede poured the wine of the gods, Apollo played his harp, and even Aphrodite was caught up in the general merrymaking and was happy with her son and new daughter-in-law.

In due time Psyche bore a daughter whose name was Pleasure.

Psyche's last task represents the most profound step of personal growth for a woman. Few people are sufficiently developed to begin such a task and it would be foolhardy to undertake such a journey unless the preceding tasks have been accomplished. To try such a journey too early is to invite disaster; to refuse the task if it is presented is equally terrible. In earlier times this was seldom attempted by ordinary people. It was left to the elect of the spiritual world. Today more and more women are called to this step of evolution. It generates power within them whether they know it or not. What is important is choosing to begin this process when it arises. You can not ignore this process once it begins any more than you can ignore pregnancy.

What do we learn from our story?

Each of first three helpers was a natural element—ant, reed, eagle. The tower is man-made and represents the cultural legacy of our civilization. It helps so much to know what other women have done in earlier times with their fourth task. St. Theresa of Avila speaks of it as the Interior Castle. The leaders of Theosophy, mostly women, have their view of it. The feminists of our time have much to say. The stories of women saints in Christian legend provide more material. Jungian psychology has produced several chronicles of women's ways. It is exceedingly important to discern the earlier ways, both eastern and western, and their differences from our contemporary path. Finally, as with most things, you are left with your own interior tower and solitary way.

Psyche must make her way into the underworld through the place of waste, (how many journeys begin at the least expected or valued place), down the pathless way into the dark recesses of the inner world. She must not stop on the way and must not be drawn aside by her generosity or her usual feminine kindness. Otherwise she will be exhausted and stranded. She pays her way across the river Styx with a coin. If she does not have enough energy stored up at the beginning of the journey she will not have the means of accomplishing it. This journey requires rest, solitude, an accumulation of energy. She must divert the terrible dog which guards the gates of Hades. There is no ignoring the vicious things one finds; they must be paid off with something of their own kind—barley cakes made with honey.

Next it is important not to dispel the energy for the

journey by settling in with Persephone and adopting her ways. It would also abort the journey. Persephone is queen of the underworld, the most hidden of all the goddesses, eternal maiden, queen of mysteries. This part of a woman must be honored and respected for it is here that the mystery is to be found; but you may not identify with it. It is not difficult to find examples of women who remained with Persephone and made no further development.

Psyche makes her way back from Hades, distracts the terrible dog long enough to get by him, pays the ferryman with a coin, and returns to the human world of light.

Psyche asks for a cask of beauty ointment but receives—to her eyes—nothing. That nothing is called the secret mystery and is probably more valuable than any quality for which we could find a name. The deepest interior mystery for a woman may not be named or given any label. It is the essence of that feminine quality which must remain a mystery, certainly to men, and hardly less so for women. It is not less than the element of healing itself.

When Psyche disobeys (another felix culpa, a fall from grace which is necessary for drama to unfold?) she takes the divine feminine element for her own use and is made unconscious by it. This is the most dangerous moment of the journey and many people fail here. To identify with the mystery is to lapse into unconsciousness, which is the end of any further development. Many women who safely make the journey this far fall into the trap of identifying with Persephone's mysterious charm. No further development is possible to them, and they remain a kind of spiritual fossil with no human dimension.

Psyche would have failed at this test, but her failure activates Eros, or her interior masculine side, into his masculine power and he comes to rescue her. It is the prick of an arrow of love which awakens her and redeems her from her sleep of death. Only love can save you from the hardness and remoteness of a partial spirituality.

Eros performs his godlike task and Psyche is welcomed into heaven as an immortal. Her contact with Eros has been difficult and dangerous but it finally brings immortality to Psyche, herself. Finally, you discover your own archetypal nature, that which is beyond any personal dimension. You then participate in the immortality which has been promised from the very beginning of the myth although in such dark and difficult terms. It was Psyche's work which translated the naive beauty promised at first into the conscious goddesshood accomplished at the end of the story.

A Modern Psyche

It is very easy to relegate mythology to a far away place long ago and thus isolate it from the mainstream of here-and-now life. It is only recently in our history that we have taken the attitude that myths and fairy stories belong to the children. Before Enlightenment attitudes prevailed, myth and story were considered a dignified and worthy subject for adult study and appreciation. It is only with the work of Jung, Fraser, Campbell, and others that myth has begun to regain its proper place in our study of the inner world; but the nineteenth century attitudes toward myth still prevail with most people.

A MODERN DREAM

Let us look at mythology at work in our own time and discover that Psyche is still working at her evolution and addressing her "tasks."

The following is a dream of a modern woman, a true Psyche, who is working at her task of the evolution of consciousness using the setting of our own time and the language of our own American culture. She is in her 30s, married, with children and a profession, and is working at full capacity with the modern urban things which surround anyone immersed in our contemporary society. As Psyche used her ancient setting as the stage for her drama, so this woman is using the contemporary world as grist for the mill of her evolution. Myth is not confined to any time or place or language.

Here is her dream:

> I found myself in a lovely, old, large and mostly empty house. I was cleaning and fixing it up with a few other people. My section to clean was on the second floor. I climbed up a broad staircase that turned to the right and walked straight ahead to "my" room. But as I stepped through the doorway I suddenly found myself in another world. It was as if I had stepped through a portal to another time and space. I was in a gorgeous high mountainside. Everything was white. It took a few minutes to realize that I was not cold at all and that the whiteness around me was not snow but some strange and mysterious substance. This

substance was luminous. There was a man there to greet me. His name was X and he spoke with a thick Slavic accent. He was about my age and size and had a thin beard. He was a lovely man, gentle yet seductive. He invited me to come with him to explore this beautiful place. I wanted so much to go with him and yet I feared that if I moved about at all in this world I would lose the reality of the house and the world as I knew it. I felt compelled to return. He understood and said that he would always be there for me when I returned. With this he turned me around and pointed the way back through the portal. I was jolted back into the house.

There were sounds downstairs, people moving things in. I rushed down the stairs and passed B. (another person who was cleaning) on the way. He said nothing but gave me a sly grin that made me feel terribly uneasy. As I was trying to sort out just what was happening I caught a glimpse of a woman with white, shoulder length hair. She walked by and disappeared. I heard someone refer to her as "Millie" and say that she was going into the other world. I ran after her, frantic to ask her what she knew but all I could get were glimpses of her as she turned a corner. I followed her up the stairs and down a long hallway and into a room. When I reached the room she was gone, vanished by choice into another world!

I started back downstairs but as I passed my room I was thrown into the white world again. X was there with a friend and said that they had been waiting for me. He gave me a long warm kiss and showed me a vehicle that was to drive me about. I felt so confused. I wanted to go with him and yet I had the distinct impression that if I did there would be no going back. I turned from him in trying to decide and in the next moment found myself back in my room in the house.

I went back downstairs. It was full of commotion. There are people moving things into the house, furniture, food, everything. A large crowd had gathered in the livingroom. I stepped into a small parlor and saw my Buddhist teacher there. She was quietly sitting in a small chair in the corner of the room in her brown robes. I had a sense then of the house being full of portals like the one I discovered. I thought that as people filled the house with themselves and their things the portals would fade. I was overcome with a sense of urgency to decide what to do before my portal was taken over by the crowd. I tried to explain my dilemma to my teacher but she spoke very little. I paced about the room and stared at all the things that filled the room. My attention fell on a blue pincushion that sat on a small table. It was as if I was trying to memorize all the details of this world to carry with me into the other. At some point I bolted out of the room and ran up the stairs intent on finding X again. I leapt through the doorway and felt the shift to the white world and woke up a second later.

I fell back asleep and re-dreamt this dream in exact detail twice more that night. Each time the sequence of events was the same except that with each dream the house became more crowded with people and things and X and the other world became more alluring.

When you have a large dream it is like a myth and carries much of the power and impact of the great myths that we are accustomed to viewing so impersonally. A Hindu friend of mine, when I had shown him the power of the dreams he had access to, exclaimed, "Here I have been, sitting on God all of my life and I did not know it!" True; God and his language of mythology are closer to all of us than our modern mind knows.

Our dream is the myth for this particular modern woman and it is fascinating to see how much it conforms to the pattern of Eros and Psyche and how much it differs. We contain (or does it contain us?) the same psychological structure as someone who lived two and a half millenniums ago; but it is also true that much evolution has gone on in that span of time. Our modern myth records the awe-inspiring sameness of human structure, but also portrays a specific focus that is uniquely modern. Each detail of the dream is worth observing in this light.

The problem of Eros and Psyche could be condensed into a single word—levels. All of the journeys, tasks and struggles of Psyche are better understood by levels. She is thrown about between earth and heaven, mortality and immortality, humanness and godliness. It is the ultimate synthesis of these opposites which is Psyche's victory. All of her struggles are to reconcile the many levels which play upon her.

The same urgency of levels appears in our modern dream. Note how many times the dreamer goes up or down the stairs! And the whole dream revolves around the interplay between the ordinary world and the white world of the spirit. Human people and situations make an interplay with divine characters. Psyche, two and a half millenniums ago and now, too, is struggling to be the mediator between these many levels. The determined look on the face of any modern mother chauffeuring her children to their afternoon appointment is a modern Psyche poised between the two worlds of her love and the avalanche of practicality which is our modern life. Psyche's tasks have changed only in detail.

A woman can awaken on a particular day and encounter beauty and numinosity but she does not know whether to give thanks for such an epiphany or to implore the gods to go back where they belong and leave her to the human tasks of the day. Eros can suddenly whisk you away into his luminous world and leave you wondering how many more stop lights you can cope with. It is exactly this collision which is the true myth! To fail either of these levels is to fail the evolutionary process at work deep within.

Our modern Psyche is immediately faced with tasks; this implies that much of the ancient myth is already accomplished for her. She has been through the specialness and isolation of her adolescence, her marriage which was such a double-edged sword, the lighting of the lamp, the loss of innocence—all of this is accomplished. The dream begins with her tasks—sorting and cleaning in her two-level house and being subjected to the sudden intrusion of the visionary world. There seems to be a great urgency in the inner world now to bridge the two worlds of heaven and earth. If only heaven would wait until the children are grown or until life has settled a little! But heaven shows no signs of waiting. She is jerked from the world of practicality into the white world of vision—and terrified that if she explores that world she will not find her way back into the practical time-space world. This is a severe danger and it is easy to fall into the trap of the either-or mentality. Dr. Jung once said that medieval man lived by either-or, but that modern people have to live either-and-or. A truly modern person can not go off to a convent or the Himalayas exclusively to search for spirituality; nor can she pour herself exclusively into her family, profession, and practicality. It is the prime task of a truly modern mind to endure both the spiritual and the practical as the framework for her life. Our dreamer does this bravely and has dreamed her masterpiece as expression of this either-and-or.

The dream is unfinished—as it should be since she has not yet reached the midpoint of her life. It will take another half lifetime to draw it to a synthesis and to bring the earth and heaven elements to a workable conclusion. The promise from the old myth is that a daughter is born—whose name is Pleasure. When one has grown strong and wise enough, the warring elements which cost so much suffering and anxiety, will become complementary elements and produce the great work of art which is your own life.

SUGGESTIONS FOR FURTHER READING

Bolen, Jean Shinoda. *Goddesses in Everywoman.* San Francisco: Harper & Row, 1985.

De Castillego, Irene C. *Knowing Woman.* New York: Harper & Row, 1974.

Grant, Toni. *Being a Woman.* New York: Random House, 1988.

Grinnell, Robert. *Alchemy in a Modern Woman.* New York: Spring Publications, 1973.

Harding, M. Esther. *The Way of All Women.* New York: Harper & Row, 1975.

Layard, John. *The Virgin Archetype.* New York: Spring Publications, 1972.

Leonard, Linda Schierse. *On the Way to the Wedding.* Boston: Shambhala, 1986.

Lewis, C. S. *Till We Have Faces.* New York: Harcourt Brace, 1957.

Neumann, Erich. *Amor and the Psyche.* Princeton: Princeton University Press, 1971.

Von Franz, Marie-Louise. *Problems of the Feminine in Fairytales.* New York: Spring Publications, 1972.

Weaver, Rix. *The Old Wise Woman.* New York: G.P. Putnam's Sons, 1973.

Woodman, Marion. *The Pregnant Virgin.* Toronto, Inner City Books, 1985.